Ballynahinch Postcards

Poems by PETER FALLON

GW00985969

○
_____

Occasional Press

In collaboration with
Ballynahinch Castle Hotel

Ballynahinch Postcards
was first published
as a collaboration between
Ballynahinch Castle Hotel
and
Occasional Press
in June 2007
in a limited signed edition of
185 numbered hardback copies
and 1000 paperback copies.

Occasional Press
Aghabullogue
Co. Cork
Ireland

www.occasionalpress.net

Poems © Peter Fallon
Cover Painting © Basil Blackshaw and Peter Fallon

Paperback: ISBN 978-0-9548976-6-6
Hardback: ISBN 978-0-9548976-5-9

for Alice

The god of life is accident.

— John McGahern

Azaleas: Hilary's House

They are the pale
refugees
of Spring —
these buds that push
against the window
opening

on a sheltered nook.
Beyond, midwinter duskus
is a glowering.
But they, they cuddle to
the pane and reimburse
its warmth by January flowering.

Chatelaine

A winter night
as bright as midnight
in mid-June

a passing cloud
bestows
the curtsy of the moon.

■

Sunset on the river,
gold frame around

a single cloud.

Still lake and river ripple —

the antics of an otter
possessed the whole morning.

Party of One

A green leaf tablecloth
is set

with a plate
of elderberry petals.

Cue

You walk most mornings
in the wood
beside the river.
So far, *so* good.

And then —
on cue —
a bird erupts
to give the day its due.

■

Look out.
Another sentry.

A crow high in
the crow's nest

of Scots Pine,
his cry calls for

a drop of oil,
his stuck record

scratches his
'No Entry'.

■

The sudden shock
of meeting them,
dressed to kill.

Then the muffled cries
across a hill
of beaters flushing woodcock,

staccato farts of fowlers' guns.

■

A new-born foal
finding its feet
in the infield;

dun ponies
paddling
in the shallows

of the longer grasses.

A piper conjured
Easter snows
out of the blossoms
of the sloes.

■

A swarm of starlings
tumbling
cartwheels in the air,

head over heels
in love
with there,

and here, and now.

Late

Just like that —
cloud cover blows up
and away.
   Two days after
my return
Ben Lettery shows up.

■

A cloud's curtain
swished
across a mountain lake —

a blink,
a wink
of its one eye.

■

Three mountainy ewes
at grass

on the upper deck
of the mountain

swept overboard
by the fury of flash floods

and pushed and pulled downward
to snag below the falls —

their vacant sockets like
the smudged mascara on the eyes

of a burnt-out holiday home
tucked behind a quiet chapel.

■

Sharp frost. Bright sun.
The sky all blue.

Wind runs
its fingers through

the long hair
of the waterfall.

A Visiting

I'd been keeping my eyes on
the reeds and rushes,
the bens straddling the horizon,

when I won
my reward — in just one day a hare
and hawk, a waterhen and heron.

■

That heron in the flooded field
a sentry —

a smudge of smoke
taking off and taking shape,

at once
tenant kind and gentry.

■

A day so still
the stones belie
their history —

by the gable of a long
abandoned cottage
a crippled tree

whose apples grew
on a branch
in Eden.

■

They have turned
their backs to the wind,
trees in that stand,
and yearn for where
the winds don't blow;

they're inclined to the East —
with their prayer mats
of fallen leaves
and all those leaves
strained to know.

A History

Like that great wall
across the Burren

this straggle
on a barren

slope the fruit
of long labours —

a lost cause now
to keep

one man's stones
out from his neighbours'.

■

They weigh
on you, the sins
of the world,
on such a day

you couldn't
rightly say
where mist ends
and cloud begins.

■

Rumpled lake,
river rush —
let all our tears

be washed away
like riffles at
forgiving weirs.

■

I'd begun to think
the like of this
might never strike
again,
the dance of days
in their rightful place.

And when we wanted
music,
there it was —
the rain.

'God Beams'

1

Cloud cover
sprawls across
the stretches
of the bog —
its splinters

form a monstrance,
laughter on
your children's faces,
the hand of kindness
proffered from a fog.

2

A welding torch
burns its way
through the steel
of cloud cover —

its glare the hub,
its light fingers
spokes
of plenty's wheel.

Is it any wonder
the tip of Ben Lettery
gleams and glows,

what with the glitter
of a lake lapping
and tickling its toes?

■

I had waited an age
to see this winter bush
again, all life
but little foliage,

a paradigm
of active peace,
where nothing happens
all the time.

■

Here a ben,
there a reek —

anywhere
a mountain peak.

You wake and wonder
if it's waiting

or if it's begun already,
the daily play

of hide-and-seek.

Daylight Robbery

You think you'll dander out
to look at the mountain
and find yourself venturing out
to look *for* the mountain.

Geography

When I looked
at the mountain
long enough
I grew to know
all manner
of mountains.

On Air

I heard a music
last night by the river.
Ethereal.

The strings of angels'
instruments
aren't real.

The Morning News

You wake up wondering
if Mikey's heifer
calved last night,
a full week beyond her time.

Devotions

Dawn dilutes the dark.
I stand beside
the glistening
current,
listening.

I must take more time
to learn from rivers.

One World

Nearly two days after
the tsunami

an extra ripple where
the river bumps against the sea.

Squall

A flock of seabirds
blown to bits —

confetti where
waves wed the shore.

Isadora

The tide
breathes in, breathes out,
breathes in again.

The beach is basking
in the sea's attention.

She said,
I learned to dance
by watching waves.

Storm

A storm
is happening to the shore. Growls
in the stomach of the surge.
Slaps and smashes. A mastiff's howls.

You,
who'd beware a quiet bull
yet needed to test everything,
could not resist the ocean's pull.

Morning, and the winds
abate.
You leave the mad hounds of the gale
tethered to the garden gate.

Grey

World of wonders.
The slightest shift
of season —
cloud, sunshine,
sun showers, a breeze on

a clear day...
                    And she'd
to ask, Why live?
Would she had seen
each of these
could be a reason.

Sea Side

A field day for gulls
in the waves
in the wake of a plow.

■

A petrel walks
        upon the water.
Breakers ripple
        their applause.

Rockfall

Some breakers spend
themselves
and slump towards rockfall.

Some bang
their heads
against the wall

of the headland's end.
The squeal and squall
of a seabird

you can't see, the all
of it the part of us
calling to be heard.

Chough

How he works his way
high
into the wind —

furl, tack, gybe
or trim,
our homebound

sailor of the sky.

Pibroch

Above the din
a medley of wind music
traced along stretched wire
to the font —

the hollow bar of a broken gate.
I played my fingers
on the stops of that salt-rusted hole
and tracked a slow air from beyond.

■

'Cheerleaders by the Road
to Clifden, with Pompoms' —
clumps of winter reeds
and grasses

rehearse their flustered repertoire
of Mexican waves
as a fleet of supertankers
passes.

Gurteen

A seaside cemetery
far to the west.
The kin of part-time fishermen,
small farmers, tradesmen,
a duchess from the 'House', all laid to rest.

And lost to sight. In the bite
of winds and rains
a fishing net restrains
sods and clods, wreaths
and withered flowers: earthly remains.

A Brighter Blue (Postscript)

At home they've rowed the barley straw
they'll aim to bale today;
so long now since
green May.

For darkening days
are here again,
more than mist,
not quite rain.

And there's a spell
I'd wanted to persist —
though times push past
as the minutes, days and weeks insist.

But who lives in the real
world? So quicken it anew.
Return, replace, repair,
reconstitute, renew.

Turn up the sun!
And put the leaves back
on the trees.
Let river reins hang slack.

Wash the sky
a brighter blue.
Give back to swans
their downy retinue.

Add notes
to summer birds' refrain.
Re-ignite the embers
of rhododendron, Golden Rain.

Resurrect, resuscitate.
Refresh and renovate.
Retrieve, regain and re-install,
translate

everything again. Restore
light moments to the day —
nothing can steal
this while away.

Acknowledgements

It is a truth that, were it not for the kindness of Ed Downe, a sponsor of art here and in the US, these poems would not have come into being.

Once upon a time when I needed a bolt-hole and was offered a residency in Monaco (a place which meant all but nothing to me) Ed opened the door of Hilary's House on the step of Ballynahinch Castle (a place I've loved since I stumbled on it one wet and weathery night in the summer of 1977). In the years since that offer my annual winter 'retreats' and other visits, including occasional stays with friends in the different splendours of the Castle itself, have been an excitement and a sustenance. These sojourns have bestowed respite from the rigours of my involvement in the editing and compilation of books by other writers. They helped me complete my translation *The Georgics of Virgil* (2004) and many of the poems in my forthcoming *The Company of Horses* (2007), as well as all of the glances and glimpses in this edition. And so, to my friend Ed, his wife Mary, and his daughter Hilary, I tender sincere thanks for a haven.

I owe debts of gratitude also to other welcomers at and around Ballynahinch: Patrick O'Flaherty, Mikey Conneely and Noel King; also John Fanning and Brendan Flynn and, for their unwavering good cheer, Bríd and Freddie and Marion in the hotel. Particular thanks are due to my dear friends, and guardians of Ben Lettery — Clare and Des Lally.

Peter Fallon,
Loughcrew

February 2007